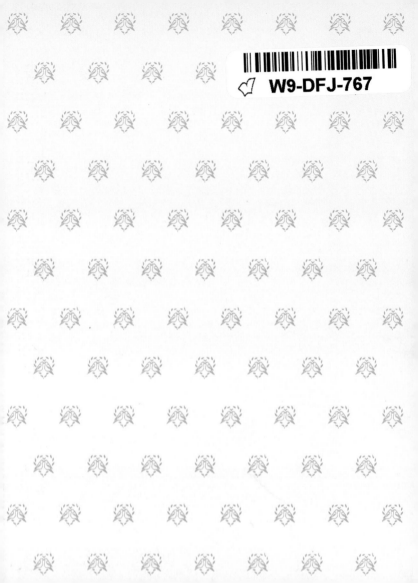

♉ LOVE SIGNS ♉

TAURUS

April 21 – May 21

JULIA & DEREK PARKER

♥ ♥

DK

Dedicated to Martin Lethbridge

A D K P U B L I S H I N G B O O K

Project Editor • Annabel Morgan
Art Editor • Anna Benjamin
Managing Editor • Francis Ritter
Managing Art Editor • Derek Coombes
DTP Designer • Cressida Joyce
Production Controller • Martin Croshaw
US Editor • Constance M. Robinson

A C K N O W L E D G M E N T S

Photography: Steve Gorton: pp. 10, 13–15, 17–19, 46–49; Ian O'Leary: 16. *Additional photography by:* Colin Keates, David King, Monique Le Luhandre, David Murray, Tim Ridley, Clive Streeter, Harry Taylor, Matthew Ward. *Artworks:* Nic Demin: 34–45; Peter Lawman: *jacket*, 4, 12; Paul Redgrave: 24–33; Satwinder Sehmi: *glyphs*; Jane Thomson: *borders*; Rosemary Woods: 11.

Peter Lawman's paintings are exhibited by the Portal Gallery Ltd, London.

Picture credits: Bridgeman Art Library/Hermitage, St. Petersburg: 51; Robert Harding Picture Library: 20l, 20c, 20r; Images Colour Library: 9; The National Gallery, London: 11; The Natural History Museum, London: 49br; The Royal Geographical Society: 48br; Tony Stone Images: 21t, 21b; The Victoria and Albert Museum, London: 5; Zefa: 21c.

ISBN 0-7894-1090-7

Reproduced by Bright Arts, Hong Kong
Printed and bound by Imago, Hong Kong

CONTENTS

ASTROLOGY & YOU

THERE IS MUCH MORE TO ASTROLOGY THAN YOUR SUN SIGN.
A SIMPLE INVESTIGATION INTO THE POSITION OF THE OTHER
PLANETS AT THE MOMENT OF YOUR BIRTH WILL PROVIDE YOU
WITH FASCINATING INSIGHTS INTO YOUR PERSONALITY.

*Y*our birth sign, or Sun sign, is the sign of the zodiac that the Sun occupied at the moment of your birth. The majority of books on astrology concentrate only on explaining the relevance of the Sun signs. This is a simple form of astrology that can provide you with some interesting but rather general information about you and your personality. In this book, we take you a step further, and reveal how the planets Venus and Mars work in association with your Sun sign to influence your attitudes toward romance and sexuality.

In order to gain a detailed insight into your personality, a "natal" horoscope, or birth chart, is necessary. This details the position of all the planets in our solar system at the moment of your birth, not just the position of the Sun. Just as the Sun occupied one of the 12 zodiac signs when you were born, perhaps making you "a Geminian" or "a Sagittarian," so each of the other planets occupied a certain sign. Each planet governs a different area of your personality, and the planets Venus and Mars are responsible for your attitudes toward love and sex, respectively.

For example, if you are a Sun-sign Sagittarian, according to the attributes of the sign you should be a dynamic, freedom-loving character. However, if Venus occupied Libra when you were born, you may make a passive and clinging partner – qualities that are supposedly completely alien to Sagittarians.

A MAP OF THE CONSTELLATION

*The 16th-century astronomer Copernicus first made the
revolutionary suggestion that the planets orbit the Sun
rather than Earth. In this 17th-century constellation chart,
the Sun is shown at the center of the solar system.*

The tables on pages 52–61 of
this book will enable you to
discover the positions of Mars
and Venus at the moment of
your birth. Once you have read
this information, turn to pages
22–45. On these pages we
explain how the influences of
Venus and Mars interact with
the characteristics of your
Sun sign. This information
will provide you with many
illuminating insights into your
personality, and explains how
the planets have formed your
attitudes toward love and sex.

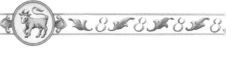

LOOKING FOR A LOVER

ASTROLOGY CAN PROVIDE YOU WITH VALUABLE INFORMATION
ON HOW TO INITIATE AND MAINTAIN RELATIONSHIPS. IT CAN
ALSO TELL YOU HOW COMPATIBLE YOU ARE WITH YOUR LOVER,
AND HOW SUCCESSFUL YOUR RELATIONSHIP IS LIKELY TO BE.

*P*eople frequently use astrology to lead into a relationship, and "What sign are you?" is often used as a conversation opener. Some people simply introduce the subject as an opening gambit, while others place great importance on this question and its answer.

Astrology can affect the way you think and behave when you are in love. It can also provide you with fascinating information about your lovers and your relationships. Astrology cannot tell you who to fall in love with or who to avoid, but it can offer you some very helpful advice.

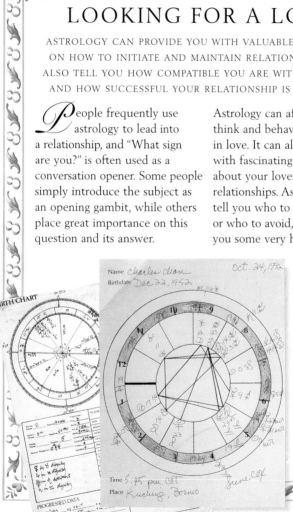

BIRTH CHARTS
Synastry involves the comparison of two people's charts in order to assess their compatibility in all areas of their relationship. The process can highlight any areas of common interest or potential conflict.

THE TABLE OF ELEMENTS

People whose signs are grouped under the same element tend to find it easy to fall into a happy relationship. The groupings are:

FIRE: *Aries, Leo, Sagittarius*
EARTH: *Taurus, Virgo, Capricorn*
AIR: *Gemini, Libra, Aquarius*
WATER: *Cancer, Scorpio, Pisces*

When you meet someone to whom you are attracted, astrology can provide you with a valuable insight into his or her personality. It may even reveal unattractive characteristics that your prospective partner is trying to conceal.

Astrologers are often asked to advise lovers involved in an ongoing relationship, or people who are contemplating a love affair. This important aspect of astrology is called synastry, and involves comparing the birth charts of the two people concerned. Each birth chart records the exact position of the planets at the moment and place of a person's birth.

By interpreting each chart separately, then comparing them, an astrologer can assess the compatibility of any two people, showing where problems may arise in their relationship, and where strong bonds will form.

One of the greatest astrological myths is that people of some signs are not compatible with people of certain other signs. This is completely untrue. Whatever your Sun sign, you can have a happy relationship with a person of any other sign.

YOU & YOUR LOVER

KNOWING ABOUT YOURSELF AND YOUR LOVER IS THE KEY TO
A HAPPY RELATIONSHIP. HERE WE REVEAL THE TRADITIONAL
ASSOCIATIONS OF TAURUS, YOUR COMPATIBILITY WITH ALL THE
SUN SIGNS, AND THE FLOWERS LINKED WITH EACH SIGN.

THE APPLE TREE
IS LINKED
WITH THE
SIGN OF
TAURUS

THE PLANET
VENUS RULES
BOTH TAURUS
AND LIBRA

THE DAISY IS
ONE OF THE
FLOWERS
RULED BY
TAURUS

APPLES, PEARS,
AND GRAPES ARE
ALL TAUREAN
FOODS

HANDSOME
TAUREANS
OFTEN HAVE
A STOCKY
BUILD

TAURUS IS
ASSOCIATED
WITH BULLS,
AND ALL
CATTLE ARE
RULED BY
THIS SIGN

TAURUS AND ARIES

You will provide Ariens with
stability and security, and Arien
sparkle and dash will liven you
up a little. You are two very
different personalities, but you
can make a good combination.

*Lavender is a
Geminian
flower*

*Thistles
are ruled
by Aries*

TAURUS AND GEMINI

Your stubborness and stolidity
could irritate a flighty Geminian,
and the flirtatiousness of Gemini
may make you possessive. If you
can overcome these problems,
you will be a happy couple.

TAURUS AND TAURUS

Two slow and steady Taureans
are in danger of slipping into
an unvarying routine. If you try
to kindle a spark of excitement
in your relationship, you should
achieve a happy, secure union.

*The lily, and
other white
flowers, are
ruled by
Cancer*

*The rose is
associated
with
Taurus*

TAURUS AND CANCER

Your Taurean dependability
and reliability will appeal to an
anxious Cancerian, and you will
enjoy the feeling of security that
Cancer offers. This is a happy
and harmonious combination.

TAURUS AND LEO
Taureans and Leos are very determined to get their own way. You must both make a concerted effort to compromise, or your alliance could degenerate into a power struggle.

*Hydrangeas
are governed by Libra*

TAURUS AND LIBRA
You both enjoy the luxuries of life, and will work hard to create a happy and harmonious relationship and a cozy, comfortable home. Do not allow Libran indecision to irritate you.

*Sunflowers
are ruled
by Leo*

TAURUS AND VIRGO
This is a perfect combination of two warm earth signs. Taurean steadiness is a perfect match for Virgoan practicality and reliability, and you will enjoy a sensual and rewarding sex life.

*Honeysuckle is
attributed to Scorpio*

TAURUS AND SCORPIO
Both Taurus and Scorpio are stubborn and passionate – and extremely jealous and possessive. You are a well-matched couple, and will share an intense and enduring mutual attraction.

*Small, brightly colored flowers
are associated with Virgo*

TAURUS AND SAGITTARIUS
A carefree and irresponsible
Sagittarian could find the
steadiness and stolidity of Taurus
infuriating. This pairing will only
work if you can allow Sagittarius
considerable independence.

*Orchids are
associated
with
Aquarius*

*Carnations
are ruled by
Sagittarius*

TAURUS AND AQUARIUS
Free-spirited and independent
Aquarians will firmly resist your
attempts to tie them down. As
Aquarius and Taurus are complete
opposites, you may have to look
hard to find common ground.

*Viburnum
is governed
by Pisces*

TAURUS AND CAPRICORN
Taurus and Capricorn are a
well-matched pair of earth signs.
A sensible Capricorn will calm
down a headstrong Taurean, and
your Taurean warmth will soften
a chilly Capricorn heart.

*Pansies are
Capricorn
flowers*

TAURUS AND PISCES
You will bring an element of
common sense and practicality
to sensitive, dreamy Pisceans.
In return, your Taurean warmth
and ardor will soon win a
romantic Piscean heart.

THE FOOD OF LOVE

WHEN PLANNING A SEDUCTION, THE SENSUOUS DELIGHTS OF AN
EXQUISITE MEAL SHOULD NEVER BE UNDERESTIMATED. READ ON
TO DISCOVER THE PERFECT MEAL FOR EACH OF THE SUN SIGNS,
GUARANTEED TO AROUSE INTEREST AND STIR DESIRE.

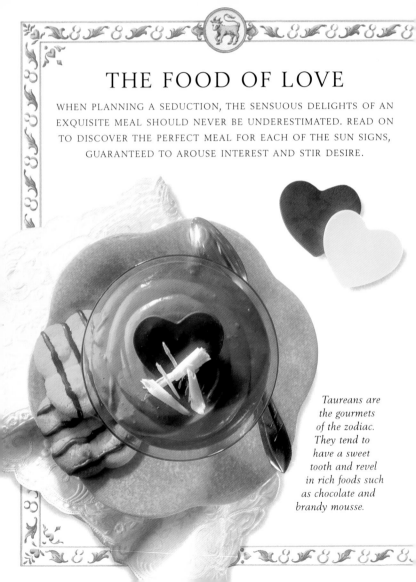

*Taureans are
the gourmets
of the zodiac.
They tend to
have a sweet
tooth and revel
in rich foods such
as chocolate and
brandy mousse.*

– THE FOOD OF LOVE –

FOR ARIENS

Spicy mulligatawny soup
·
Peppered steak
·
Baked Alaska

FOR TAUREANS

Cream of cauliflower soup
·
Tournedos Rossini
·
Rich chocolate and brandy mousse

FOR GEMINIANS

Seafood and avocado salad
·
Piquant stir-fried pork with ginger
·
Zabaglione

FOR CANCERIANS

Artichoke vinaigrette
·
Sole Bonne Femme
·
Almond soufflé

- THE FOOD OF LOVE -

FOR LEOS
Roasted tomato and garlic soup
·
Boeuf Stroganoff
·
Pears cooked in wine

FOR VIRGOS
Eggplant salad
·
Paella
·
French apple tart

FOR LIBRANS
Asparagus with hollandaise sauce
·
Pork with roasted apples
·
Strawberry Pavlova

FOR SCORPIOS
Vichyssoise
·
Lobster Newburg
·
Blueberry cream

- THE FOOD OF LOVE -

FOR SAGITTARIANS

Chilled cucumber soup

·

Nutty onion flan

·

Rhubarb crumble with fresh cream

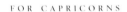

FOR CAPRICORNS

Eggs Florentine

·

Pork tenderloin stuffed with sage

·

Pineapple Pavlova

FOR AQUARIANS

Watercress soup

·

Chicken cooked with chili and lime

·

Lemon soufflé

FOR PISCEANS

French onion soup

·

Trout au vin rosé

·

Melon sorbet

PLACES TO LOVE

ONCE YOU HAVE WON YOUR LOVER'S HEART, A ROMANTIC
VACATION TOGETHER WILL SEAL YOUR LOVE. HERE, YOU
CAN DISCOVER THE PERFECT DESTINATION FOR EACH SUN
SIGN, FROM HISTORIC CITIES TO IDYLLIC BEACHES.

THE
EIFFEL
TOWER,
PARIS

ARIES

*Florence is an Arien
city, and its perfectly
preserved Renaissance
palaces and churches
will set the scene for
wonderful romance.*

TAURUS

*The unspoiled scenery
and unhurried pace
of life in rural Ireland
is sure to appeal to
patient and placid
Taureans.*

GEMINI

*Vivacious and restless
Geminians will feel at
home in the fast-paced
and sophisticated
atmosphere of
New York.*

CANCER

*The watery beauty
and uniquely romantic
atmosphere of Venice
is guaranteed to arouse
passion and stir the
Cancerian imagination.*

ST. BASIL'S
CATHEDRAL,
MOSCOW

AYERS ROCK/ULURU,
AUSTRALIA

THE PYRAMIDS,
EGYPT

LEO
Leos will fall in love all over again when surrounded by the picturesque charm and unspoiled medieval atmosphere of Prague.

VIRGO
Perhaps the most elegant and romantic of all cities, Paris is certainly the ideal setting for a stylish and fastidious Virgo.

LIBRA
The dramatic and exotic beauty of Upper Egypt and the Nile will provide the perfect backdrop for wooing a romantic Libran.

SCORPIO
Intense and passionate Scorpios will be strongly attracted by the whiff of danger present in the exotic atmosphere of New Orleans.

SAGITTARIUS
The wide-ranging spaces of the Australian outback will appeal to the Sagittarian love of freedom and the great outdoors.

CAPRICORN
Capricorns will be fascinated and inspired by the great historical monuments of Moscow, the most powerful of all Russian cities.

AQUARIUS
Intrepid Aquarians will be enthralled and amazed by the unusual sights and spectacular landscapes of the Indian subcontinent.

PISCES
Water-loving Pisceans will be at their most relaxed and romantic by the sea, perhaps on a small and unspoiled Mediterranean island.

GONDOLAS,
VENICE

THE TAJ MAHAL,
INDIA

VENUS & MARS

LUCID, SHINING VENUS AND FIERY, RED MARS HAVE ALWAYS BEEN ASSOCIATED WITH HUMAN LOVE AND PASSION. THE TWO PLANETS HAVE A POWERFUL INFLUENCE ON OUR ATTITUDES TOWARD LOVE, SEX, AND RELATIONSHIPS.

The study of astrology first began long before humankind began to record its own history. The earliest astrological artifacts discovered, scratches on bones recording the phases of the Moon, date from well before the invention of any alphabet or writing system.

The planets Venus and Mars have always been regarded as having enormous significance in astrology. This is evident from the tentative attempts of early astrologers to record the effects of the two planets on humankind. Hundreds of years later, the positions of the planets were carefully noted in personal horoscopes. The earliest known record is dated 410 BC: "Venus [was] in the Bull, and Mars in the Twins."

The bright, shining planet Venus represents the gentle effect of the soul on our physical lives. It is responsible for a refined and romantic sensuality – "pure" love, untainted by sex. Venus reigns over our attitudes toward romance and the spiritual dimension of love.

The planet Mars affects the physical aspects of our lives – our strength, both physical and mental; our endurance; and our ability to fight for survival. Mars is also strongly linked to the sex drive of both men and women. Mars governs our physical energy, sexuality, and levels of desire.

Venus is known as an "inferior" planet, because its orbit falls between Earth and the Sun. Venus orbits the Sun

LOVE CONQUERS ALL

In Botticelli's Venus and Mars, *the warlike, fiery
energy of Mars, the god of war, has been overcome by
the gentle charms of Venus, the goddess of love.*

closely, and its position in the
zodiac is always in a sign near
that of the Sun. As a result, the
planet can only have occupied
one of five given signs at the
time of your birth – your Sun
sign, or the two signs before or
after it. For example, if you were
born with the Sun in Virgo,
Venus can only have occupied
Cancer, Leo, Virgo, Libra, or
Scorpio at that moment.

Mars, on the other hand, is
a "superior" planet. Its orbit lies
on the other side of Earth from
the Sun, and therefore the
planet may have occupied any
of the 12 signs at the moment
of your birth.

On the following pages
(24–45) we provide you with
fascinating insights into how
Mars and Venus govern your
attitudes toward love, sex, and
relationships. To ascertain which
sign of the zodiac the planets
occupied at the moment of
your birth, you must first consult
the tables on pages 52–61. Then
turn to page 24 and read on.

YOUR LOVE LIFE

THE PLANET VENUS REPRESENTS LOVE, HARMONY, AND UNITY.
WORK OUT WHICH SIGN OF THE ZODIAC VENUS OCCUPIED AT
THE MOMENT OF YOUR BIRTH (SEE PAGES 52–57), AND READ ON.

VENUS IN PISCES

From Pisces, Venus will enable you to express your deepest emotions in a gentle and heartfelt fashion. Potential partners are likely to capitulate after a single glance from your soulful eyes, especially since you are likely to possess the good looks and charm typical of those born with the Sun in Taurus.

You will display the usual Taurean determination to enjoy your love life and to ensure that your partner enjoys it too. Do not devote yourself to your partner to such an extent that you become a doormat. Your lover is unlikely to object to this trait initially, but you should make an effort to repress an overwhelming desire to please, or it could become irritating.

Emotional security assumes a position of great importance in your life. You may be prone to feelings of insecurity and need to feel stable within your relationship. Try to believe your partner's ardent declarations of love for you. You are a most considerate and loving companion, and your lover will not have any reason to feel dissatisfied with you.

Despite your occasional feelings of self-doubt, this placing will curb the natural possessiveness that Venus can bring from Taurus. You are not likely to become clinging or overly dependent on your partner; therefore, the atmosphere should not become restrictive or claustrophobic.

From Taurus, the Sun will bring you a love of luxury and comfort, and as a result you tend to be rather extravagant. At first, your lover may enjoy being pampered and spoiled, but your lavish spending may worry a permanent partner. Do not be offended if he or she suggests that you should tighten your belt, for your partner may have a more realistic view of your financial situation than you.

From Pisces, Venus can suggest that you take the easy way out of difficult situations. You are kindhearted, so you hate hurting people's feelings or being involved in unpleasant situations. You may even lie to get yourself off the hook. If this becomes a habit, it can lead to evasiveness and deceit. Try to be honest and straightforward, and to keep the lines of communication open with your fortunate partner.

VENUS IN ARIES

*W*hen Venus is in Aries a feisty quality enters the Taurean personality and adds a little fieriness to the character. This is generally a beneficial influence, but it can cause a propensity to sudden rages. Many Taureans have a hot temper once they are aroused, and the smoldering Arien influence will increase your tendency to flare up. Try to control your temper and to prevent any sudden explosions. If you feel on the verge of blowing your top, remember that it is the influence of Venus that is provoking you. Your sudden outbursts can be disturbing, especially for your partner.

From Aries, Venus will heighten your emotions, and in some situations you may overreact in a very emotional way. Problems can be caused by your Taurean possessiveness, despite the fact that you know that you are creating an uncomfortably restrictive atmosphere. You must overcome these feelings of possessiveness, or they may grow out of proportion, damaging an otherwise happy partnership. Although you are generous in your desire to please your partner, you may possess a streak of Arien selfishness, which can interfere with your typical Taurean determination to make life as delightful as possible.

Due to the impulsive influence of Aries, you may fall passionately in love virtually instantaneously, often on the basis of physical attraction alone. You like to take the initiative, but will expect your passion to be warmly reciprocated by the object of your desire. If your overtures do not meet with an enthusiastic response, a potential lover, even an extremely attractive one, will be dropped

with alarming rapidity. Venus may make you eager to become physically involved early in a relationship, but your lover may not be quite so impetuous. Listen to your prudent Taurean instincts, rather than the hasty and impatient qualities of Aries.

You are enthusiastic, quick-witted, and adventurous, and will make a delightful and devoted partner. However, you are a very physical person, as well as a true romantic, and your long-term relationships are unlikely to prosper unless you and your partner have similar sexual appetites.

Try not to overwhelm any potential lovers with your romantic and impetuous Arien ardor. If you encourage someone to fall deeply in love with you, they may be distraught if you finally decide that, after all, they are not quite right for you.

VENUS IN TAURUS

*W*hen both Venus and the Sun occupy Taurus, all your good qualities – as well as your faults – will be emphasized. You will make an ideal partner for the right person, as all your tender and loving Taurean qualities will be underlined by this planetary placing. As a result, you will be a warm, affectionate, sensual, and romantic lover.

The qualities you display as a lover are excellent, but there are a few danger zones to watch out for. Unlikely as it may seem, some problems may stem from your physical appearance. Taureans tend to be physically attractive, and most people will also react favorably to your considerable charm. You are likely to have a constant stream of admirers, which may make you rather complacent and lazy when it comes to seeking prospective partners.

Perhaps because you are so used to being pursued, you tend to be rather passive when it comes to initiating relationships. However, your warm receptivity to affectionate overtures should reassure your lover about his or her desirability.

You may be cautious when it comes to forging relationships, but once you make a decision to commit yourself, you will make a very supportive and faithful lover. In return, you will expect your partner to be equally loyal and loving to you.

There is a danger that you may be possessive, constantly demanding time and attention from your lover. You may even become irrationally suspicious about the most innocent situations. You must try to control this tendency to cling to your partner, or a claustrophobic atmosphere may begin to pervade your relationship.

Those born with Venus in Taurus tend to have a rather sluggish metabolism. You may become lethargic and idle, so you must make sure that your enjoyment of good food does not lead to your splendid Taurean body getting out of shape.

The double influence of the Sun and Venus may intensify your Taurean preoccupation with emotional and financial security. You cannot function satisfactorily if you do not feel secure in these respects. Your partner must be sympathetic to these feelings of insecurity and understand your need for constant reassurance.

You will make an attractive and affectionate companion, and should not find it difficult to attract both friends and lovers. If you can control your possessive streak, your relationships should all be happy and harmonious.

VENUS IN GEMINI

*W*hen Venus shines from the vivacious sign of Gemini, the planet will sharpen your passionate emotions and intensify your natural charm. It will also diminish less desirable Taurean attributes such as possessiveness and lethargy.

In addition to your Taurean charm and good looks, you will be eloquent and quick-witted, and will find it easy to get acquainted with someone you are attracted to. You are a good communicator and will be completely open about your feelings. The loquacious Geminian influence will make you very persuasive; you will convincingly talk your way out of any complicated and difficult situations.

This planetary placement could make you easily bored and naturally restless. The dangerous thrill of infidelity could offer a distraction, and you may enter into clandestine affairs. Remember that illicit liaisons could damage your relationship. If your misdemeanors are discovered by your partner, an irreplaceable element of trust could vanish from your relationship forever.

In a relationship, friendship and cameraderie with your lover is very important to you. If you and your partner are close friends as well as lovers, you are less likely to develop itchy feet, and any tendency toward infidelity will be held at bay.

From Gemini, Venus may bring a hint of coolness to your personality, but your Taurean warmth should easily overcome any diffidence. Indeed, you are likely to make a very talented and sensual lover. Taurean passivity will be enlivened by Geminian vivacity, yet you will take your time and adopt a leisurely approach.

The Geminian influence is guaranteed to alleviate any less attractive Taurean personality traits, such as possessiveness and jealousy. Even the thought of these qualities may be quite repugnant to you, and you will also dislike them in a partner. However, it will be easy for you to recognize and deal with the symptoms of both jealousy and possessiveness if you are prey to these difficult emotions.

From Gemini, Venus may bring a yearning for novelty and variety. As a result, you will be more eager to try new activities than many Taureans. You relish stimulating conversation and debate, and are attracted to articulate, communicative types. You will have no difficulty in discussing your feelings and will expect your partner to be equally forthcoming about his or her emotions.

VENUS IN CANCER

*V*enus in Cancer will increase your capacity for sensual and spiritual love and affection. You are a loyal and supportive friend as well as lover, and are happy to lavish unstinting love and affection on your fortunate partner.

Due to the Cancerian influence, you will be a devoted homemaker, and much of your time and energy will be focused on your domestic life and your family. You are very protective of your partner, and attentive to his or her needs. Indeed, you can adopt an almost parental attitude toward your lover, and love to feed and pamper this person. A secure relationship is of great importance to you – almost a necessity. As a result, you will find it especially painful if your relationships break down.

The position of Venus in Cancer will raise your emotional temperature considerably.

Taureans are usually peaceful types, but you are likely to be much more volatile. You may find that you fly into a rage easily, and have a sharp and savage tongue. No relationship with you will be totally devoid of squalls, but when life is not going your way, the storm may develop into a force 10 gale. Use all your Taurean calm and Cancerian kindness to soothe yourself and subdue your hot temper.

This heightened temper may worsen any typical Taurean possessiveness. You must face up to this potential problem area and try to control it. If you suffer pangs of jealousy when you notice your lover deeply involved in conversation with someone else, mentally give yourself a stern reprimand. Even the most perfect relationships can be warped by this destructive and unpleasant emotion.

If your relationship is threatened in any way, your protective instincts will immediately go into overdrive. Even if your relationship has become a battlefield, you will still be determined to hold on to your partner with all your might. You may feel that you cannot endure life with your lover for a moment longer, but at the same time you will be loath to loosen your hold on this person.

When Venus is in Cancer, the prospect of being alone will not appeal to you, and, in addition, the influence of the planet can make you very nostalgic. You view the past through rose-colored glasses, and dislike the idea of change. This could make it difficult for you to move on in all areas of your life, but if you know in your heart of hearts that your relationship is over, you must learn to let go.

YOUR SEX LIFE

THE PLANET MARS REPRESENTS PHYSICAL AND SEXUAL ENERGY.
WORK OUT WHICH SIGN OF THE ZODIAC MARS OCCUPIED AT THE
MOMENT OF YOUR BIRTH (SEE PAGES 58–61), AND READ ON.

MARS IN ARIES

*M*ars from Aries adds passion to your Taurean sensuality. Your sex drive is increased, and your attitude toward your potent sexuality is enthusiastic and uncomplicated.

Taureans can be reserved, and often hesitate before making the first move toward someone. However, when Mars shines from Aries, you will be bolder and more impatient, particularly if your overtures are not warmly and swiftly accepted.

If your lover is indecisive, you must not bulldoze him or her into doing what you think is best. Although your motives may be the best, there is a danger that you may become domineering.

MARS IN TAURUS

*B*oth Mars and the Sun in Taurus will make you a tender, satisfying, and sensual lover. You will display high levels of sexual energy, and a generous helping of passion.

This placing of Mars can bring you a dash of jealousy and possessiveness. When combined, these two emotions may make you overreact when your partner teases you, perhaps by expressing admiration or desire for someone else. Fortunately, you are generally tolerant and equable,

and it takes a lot of provocation to rouse you to anger. However, once you do lose your temper, a dramatic explosion follows. Try to understand that your outbursts may cause serious damage, because you tend to express yourself far more aggressively than you realize.

Taureans are creatures of habit, and you must try not to become too predictable. Spice up your sex life and keep it lively by experimenting and varying your routine.

MARS IN GEMINI

*W*hen Mars shines from Gemini, you need a partner who can stimulate you both mentally and physically. If you and your lover are not both intellectually and sexually compatible, you may become irritable and frustrated.

Due to your strong Taurean sexuality, you will be particularly interested in the physical side of love. Mars in Gemini will make you eager to experiment, and your sex life should be pleasurable and exciting.

Faithfulness is not one of your strongest qualities, and there is a possibility that you may find yourself involved in more than one affair at the same time. These affairs may begin as idle flirtations, but since you are very sexual, they are likely to lead to physical involvement.

The reputation of Taurus as an exceptionally gifted and sensual lover is boosted by Mars working from Gemini, the planet that brings you physical dexterity, versatility, and energy.

MARS IN CANCER

*F*rom Cancer, Mars will bring you great powers of perseverance. When you have chosen someone, you will pursue this person with the tenacity of the bull that symbolizes your Sun sign. Your lover is indeed fortunate; for your lovemaking is intuitive and sensitive.

Due to the influence of Mars from Cancer, you will be a very loving and caring partner, but you must not smother your lover with an overabundance of affection and solicitude.

The Cancerian influence may exacerbate your hot Taurean temper. When you become involved in an argument, you can blow up suddenly and make very hurtful remarks. A little self-control could prove most valuable in this area. You may find that you bear grudges, and often feel resentful after a disagreement. You must try to banish any lingering negative emotions by openly and honestly discussing any feelings of hurt or anger with your partner.

MARS IN LEO

Taureans born with Mars in Leo will not be insulted if someone makes a pass at them. Indeed, when someone shows a romantic interest in you, you may respond with an ardor that will surprise and flatter your new admirer.

You have boundless supplies of energy, and your dynamism and sense of purpose will impress many prospective lovers. Your exuberant sex life will be equally energetic, and will be characterized by an air of fun.

Taureans live life to the fullest; and from Leo, Mars emphasizes your zest for life. Your creative mind and sense of the dramatic make you an entertaining companion, but your tendency to show off and demand attention can be tiresome.

You can be touchy and hot-tempered, but when Mars is in Leo your temper dies down as quickly as it flares up. Once an argument is over, you are quick to forgive. The concept of holding a grudge is alien to you.

MARS IN VIRGO

The influence of Mars from Virgo will not reduce your sexual appetite, but it will make you more judicious and discriminating in your choice of partners. This increased sense of perception and discernment is entirely beneficial, as it means that you will choose a permanent partner both wisely and well.

Fiery, sexually charged Mars and modest, restrained Virgo can sometimes clash. As a result, your sexuality may be slightly inhibited. Do not allow the critical influence of Virgo to repress your earthy and stimulating Taurean sexuality. Relaxation techniques, such as yoga, may relieve any nervous tension and will appeal to the sensual side of your character.

From Mars, Virgo brings high levels of intellectual energy. You must make the most of your abilities by undertaking challenging mental tasks. Remember, however, to balance hard work with sensual relaxation methods.

MARS IN LIBRA

When Mars shines from Libra, the fiery sexual energy of the planet is weakened by the languid Libran influence.

You are likely to possess a strong streak of Libran romance, and will thoroughly enjoy sighing over love poetry, pouring out your feelings in long love letters, and gazing deeply into your lover's eyes. Despite these sentimental actions, you may be rather lethargic when it comes to physically expressing your love.

The prospect of energetic sex may exhaust you, although you are an extremely sensual lover once aroused.

Try to shake off your Libran lassitude, because you do actually enjoy sex very much, and if your partner expresses pleasure and appreciation, you will reach unprecedented heights.

You will not be content with a string of casual affairs. The Libran influence will make you yearn for a satisfying long-term relationship, even when you are young and fancy free.

- YOUR SEX LIFE -

MARS IN SCORPIO

The Scorpio's reputation for sexiness is legendary, and you will possess much of this highly charged sexuality if Mars occupied Scorpio at the hour of your birth.

People with this powerful placement must express their sexuality in a satisfying way if their life is to be properly balanced. When your sexual energy does not have an outlet, there is a danger that you will become frustrated. Ultimately, if you and your partner are not sexually compatible, your long-term relationship may not be sustainable, because sex plays an important part in your life.

You have a great capacity for enjoyment, and your lovers will delight in your zest for life. You make a staunchly loyal and supportive friend and partner, but your lover may soon realize that you can also be unreasonably jealous. Do not allow this destructive emotion to get out of hand, or it may damage your relationship beyond repair.

MARS IN SAGITTARIUS

*F*rom Sagittarius, Mars encourages a lighthearted attitude to love. You have an abundance of sexual energy and enthusiasm, which you express with a seductive charm. However, try not to forget your lover's feelings in your eagerness to satisfy your own desires.

You may use your Taurean good looks to snare lovers, then drop them after a brief but enjoyable affair. Sagittarius is a restless and freedom-loving sign, with a considerable sexual appetite; therefore, you may not realize quite how much pain your behavior can cause.

Due to the influence of Mars in Sagittarius, you may believe that the grass is always greener on the other side of the fence. No matter how delightful your present companion is, you may feel that a more exciting person is just around the corner. This is rarely the case. Do not allow your roving eye to lead you into throwing away a happy and successful relationship.

MARS IN CAPRICORN

An affair with a Taurean with Mars in Capricorn can resemble a roller-coaster ride. It may be all ups and downs – intensely passionate one moment, cool and distant the next. Your Taurean charm will be enhanced by the chilly but alluring Capricorn demeanor.

When Mars shines from Capricorn, you will be naturally cautious, and may think twice before starting an affair. When you finally signal to someone that you are attracted to him or her, your courtship will be formal and restrained. Indeed, your potential lovers are likely to be tantalized by your Capricorn self-control and cool reserve.

As long as your partner understands and accepts your aloof and detached manner, you will be able to maintain a very successful relationship. You may not be a fiery and passionate lover, but you will be a constant, loyal, and faithful partner – perhaps more valuable qualities in the long term.

MARS IN AQUARIUS

*W*hen Mars is positioned in Aquarius, you may be reluctant to start a relationship, particularly if you suspect that your prospective lover is interested in a permanent commitment. You cherish your independence and personal freedom, and guard it jealously.

When you become involved in a permanent relationship, a lover who tries to keep you too closely confined will be treading on dangerous ground. When your lover treats you to a display of sentiment and affection, you may respond with an almost heartless degree of coolness due to simple defiance and fear of commitment.

When Venus shines from Aquarius, you will enjoy sex, although to describe you as passionate would be an exaggeration. You may not possess very high levels of physical energy, but you will be an exciting lover, eager to experiment and enjoy a varied and unconventional sex life.

MARS IN PISCES

*T*his placing of Mars will bring powerful emotion and a broad streak of romanticism to the Taurean expression of love. You may not be a very vigorous lover, but you will make up for this with your natural sensuality and warmth.

You love the drama of seduction and revel in the very idea of being in love. Do not completely retreat into a dream world of romantic fantasy – you must try to keep at least one foot firmly on the ground.

When you become involved in a happy sexual relationship, your emotions will be expressed in a wonderfully rewarding and open fashion. You will be prepared to make considerable sacrifices for your relationship, especially once you have found the right partner.

You are a fervent and poetic lover, with a lively and exotic sexual imagination. Do not try to repress your imagination. Instead, use it creatively to enhance your sexual drive.

TOKENS OF LOVE

ASTROLOGY CAN GIVE YOU A FASCINATING INSIGHT INTO YOUR
LOVER'S PERSONALITY AND ATTITUDE TOWARD LOVE. IT CAN
ALSO PROVIDE YOU WITH SOME INVALUABLE HINTS WHEN YOU
WANT TO CHOOSE THE PERFECT GIFT FOR YOUR LOVER.

JEWELED
HAIR CLIP

ARIES
*The head is ruled by Aries; therefore,
unusual hair accessories will be
appreciated. Sports equipment will
also please an active Arien lover.*

TABLE
TENNIS
BALLS

EMBROIDERED
CUSHION

TAURUS
*Taureans value quality over
quantity. Fine handpainted
porcelain will appeal to
your Taurean lover, as
will a plump and richly
embroidered cushion.*

LIMOGES
PORCELAIN
PILLBOX

MACADAMIA
NUTS

GEMINI
*A handsome box of exotic
nuts or Jordan almonds
will be greatly appreciated
by your Geminian lover.*

– TOKENS OF LOVE –

CHINESE
SNUFF
BOTTLE

ANTIQUE
SILVER
BOX

CANCER
*Cancerians
love to collect
unusual curios
and antiques,
particularly those
made from silver.
A print of a ship or the
ocean is also an ideal present.*

KILIM
CUSHION

LEO
*Gold is the Leo metal; therefore,
anything gold or gold-colored
is sure to appeal. Leos love
colorful, flamboyant items, and
a brightly colored cushion will
also make the perfect gift.*

GOLD
KEY RING

AFRICAN
CARVED
WOODEN
SPOON

VIRGO
*Virgos enjoy gardening,
and gardening books or
implements will always be
gratefully received. Objects
made from wood will also
appeal to your Virgoan lover.*

GARDEN
TOOLS

- TOKENS OF LOVE -

EXPENSIVE
LIPSTICK

PATTERNED
LEATHER
BELT

SCENTED
BATH
OIL

LIBRA

*Your Libran lover
revels in luxury
and elegance, and
will adore expensive
beauty products
and seductive
lingerie.*

SCORPIO

*Scorpios will be
delighted by an
attractive leather belt
or wallet. Scorpio is
a water sign, and
exotic bath products
are also guaranteed
to please your
Scorpio lover.*

SAGITTARIUS

*Adventurous, freespirited
Sagittarians love to travel,
and travel books and
accessories, such as maps
or compasses, will be
greatly appreciated.*

TRAVEL
BOOKS

ANTIQUE
COMPASS

– TOKENS OF LOVE –

CAPRICORN

*Only the best will
do for a fastidious
Capricorn. Heavy,
simply decorated
glassware, a fine
fountain pen, or a
silver picture frame
are all guaranteed
to appeal to exclusive
Capricorn tastes.*

MODERN HAND-
MADE POTTERY

AQUARIUS

*Unusual handmade
modern pottery and
glass will charm an
Aquarian, as will
glittery pieces of
costume jewelry.*

GLASS
DECANTER

CUSHION
MADE FROM
SILK SARI
MATERIAL

IRIDESCENT
GLASS
MARBLES

PISCES

*Sumptuous silks and velvets will
suit sensual Pisceans – choose
a velvet scarf or a plump cushion
for them. Iridescent glassware will
also delight your Piscean lover.*

GIVING A BIRTHSTONE

*The most personal
gift you can give
your lover is the
gem linked to his
or her Sun sign.*

EMERALD

ARIES: *diamond*
TAURUS: *emerald*
GEMINI: *agate* • CANCER: *pearl*
LEO: *ruby* • VIRGO: *sardonyx*
LIBRA: *sapphire* • SCORPIO: *opal*
SAGITTARIUS: *topaz*
CAPRICORN: *amethyst*
AQUARIUS: *aquamarine*
PISCES: *moonstone*

YOUR PERMANENT
RELATIONSHIP

TAUREANS FLOURISH WITHIN A HAPPY AND HARMONIOUS
PERMANENT RELATIONSHIP. THEY MAKE GENEROUS AND
AFFECTIONATE PARTNERS BUT CAN BE POSSESSIVE.

*H*omemaking and raising a family are high on the Taurean list of priorities, and temporary relationships are not your style. Others may enjoy the excitement of fleeting affairs, but you will be happier with a permanent alliance.

Your Taurean charm and good looks should make it easy for you to find a partner. However, it is unlikely that you will rush into a permanent arrangement, because you need to feel entirely sure of a partner before you make a commitment.

You enjoy life and will work hard to get the best out of it. While you may compromise and live on a shoestring with your partner until something better is within reach, this will not be a permanent arrangement. Settling for love in a garret will only be temporary – your ambition is to create a secure and comfortable home, and you will not be satisfied until you have achieved this aim.

Once you are on the way to making a home for yourself and your partner, you will feel increasingly positive about life. Your home will be a refuge for you and a symbol of emotional security – an aspect of life that Taureans truly value. You will work long and hard to provide your partner and your children with a secure home and the finest of material possessions.

The Taurean tendency towards overpossessiveness may cause a few problems in

On a Sailing Ship, *by Caspar David Friedrich, shows a newly married couple sailing into a bright but unknown future together.*

your permanent relationships. Do not allow your jealousy to create a stifling or claustrophobic atmosphere. The best tactic for controlling your possessive streak is to recognize its existence and try and overcome it when it rears its head.

The process of providing for your family may create difficulties. Taureans will work very hard to make a success of their careers and to become financially secure, largely to enable them to provide their families with every material possession they could desire. While this motive is an excellent one, you may find that your work occupies so much of your time that you deprive your family of your company. Do not deny yourself the pleasure of getting to know your children and enjoying time with your family.

VENUS & MARS TABLES

THESE TABLES WILL ENABLE YOU TO DISCOVER WHICH SIGNS
VENUS AND MARS OCCUPIED AT THE MOMENT OF YOUR BIRTH.
TURN TO PAGES 24–45 TO INVESTIGATE THE QUALITIES OF THESE
SIGNS, AND TO FIND OUT HOW THEY WORK WITH YOUR SUN SIGN.

*T*he tables on pages 53–61 will enable you to discover the positions of Venus and Mars at the moment of your birth.

First find your year of birth on the top line of the appropriate table, then find your month of birth in the left-hand column. Where the column for your year of birth intersects with the row for your month of birth, you will find a group of figures and zodiacal glyphs. These figures and glyphs show which sign of the zodiac the planet occupied

on the first day of that month, and any date during that month on which the planet moved into another sign.

For example, to ascertain the position of Venus on May 10, 1968, run your finger down the column marked 1968 until you reach the row for May. The row of numbers and glyphs shows that Venus occupied Aries on May 1, entered Taurus on May 4, and then moved into Gemini on May 28. Therefore, on May 10, Venus was in Taurus.

If you were born on a day when one of the planets was moving into a new sign, it may be impossible to determine your Venus and Mars signs completely accurately. If the characteristics described on the relevant pages do not seem to apply to you, read the interpretation of the sign before and after. One of these signs will be appropriate.

ZODIACAL GLYPHS

♈	Aries	♎	Libra
♉	Taurus	♏	Scorpio
♊	Gemini	♐	Sagittarius
♋	Cancer	♑	Capricorn
♌	Leo	♒	Aquarius
♍	Virgo	♓	Pisces

– VENUS TABLES –

♀	1921	1922	1923	1924	1925	1926	1927	1928
JAN	1 ♒ 7 ♓	1 ♑ 25 ♒	1 ♏ 3 ♐	1 ♒ 20 ♓	1 ♐ 15 ♑	1 ♒	1 ♑ 10 ♒	1 ♏ 5 ♐ 30 ♑
FEB	1 ♓ 3 ♈	1 ♒ 18 ♓	1 ♐ 7 ♑ 14 ♒	1 ♓ 14 ♈	1 ♑ 8 ♒	1 ♒	1 ♒ 3 ♓ 27 ♈	1 ♑ 23 ♒
MAR	1 ♈ 8 ♉	1 ♓ 14 ♈	1 ♑ 7 ♒	1 ♈ 10 ♉	1 ♒ 5 ♓ 29 ♈	1 ♒	1 ♈ 23 ♉	1 ♒ 19 ♓
APR	1 ♉ 26 ♈	1 ♈ 7 ♉	1 ♒ 2 ♓ 27 ♈	1 ♉ 8 ♊	1 ♈ 22 ♉	1 ♒ 7 ♓	1 ♉ 17 ♊	1 ♓ 12 ♈
MAY	1 ♈	1 ♉ 2 ♊ 26 ♋	1 ♈ 22 ♉	1 ♊ 7 ♋	1 ♉ 16 ♊	1 ♓ 7 ♈	1 ♊ 13 ♋	1 ♈ 7 ♉ 31 ♊
JUN	1 ♈ 3 ♉	1 ♋ 20 ♌	1 ♉ 16 ♊	1 ♋	1 ♊ 10 ♋	1 ♈ 3 ♉ 29 ♊	1 ♋ 9 ♌	1 ♊ 24 ♋
JUL	1 ♉ 9 ♊	1 ♌ 16 ♍	1 ♊ 11 ♋	1 ♋	1 ♋ 4 ♌ 29 ♍	1 ♊ 25 ♋	1 ♌ 8 ♍	1 ♋ 19 ♌
AUG	1 ♊ 6 ♋	1 ♍ 11 ♎	1 ♋ 4 ♌ 28 ♍	1 ♋	1 ♍ 23 ♎	1 ♋ 19 ♌	1 ♍	1 ♌ 12 ♍
SEP	1 ♌ 27 ♍	1 ♎ 8 ♏	1 ♍ 22 ♎	1 ♋ 8 ♌	1 ♎ 17 ♏	1 ♌ 12 ♍	1 ♍	1 ♍ 5 ♎ 30 ♏
OCT	1 ♍ 21 ♎	1 ♏ 11 ♐	1 ♎ 16 ♏	1 ♌ 8 ♍	1 ♏ 12 ♐	1 ♍ 6 ♎ 30 ♏	1 ♍	1 ♏ 24 ♐
NOV	1 ♎ 14 ♏	1 ♐ 29 ♏	1 ♏ 9 ♐	1 ♍ 3 ♎ 28 ♏	1 ♐ 7 ♑	1 ♏ 23 ♐	1 ♍ 10 ♎	1 ♐ 18 ♑
DEC	1 ♏ 8 ♐	1 ♏	1 ♐ 3 ♑ 27 ♒	1 ♏ 22 ♐	1 ♑ 6 ♒	1 ♐ 17 ♑	1 ♎ 17 ♏	1 ♑ 13 ♒

♀	1929	1930	1931	1932	1933	1934	1935	1936
JAN	1 ♒ 7 ♓	1 ♑ 25 ♒	1 ♏ 4 ♐	1 ♒ 20 ♓	1 ♐ 15 ♑	1 ♒	1 ♑ 9 ♒	1 ♏ 4 ♐ 29 ♑
FEB	1 ♓ 3 ♈	1 ♒ 17 ♓	1 ♐ 7 ♑	1 ♓ 13 ♈	1 ♑ 8 ♒	1 ♒	1 ♒ 2 ♓ 27 ♈	1 ♑ 23 ♒
MAR	1 ♈ 9 ♉	1 ♓ 13 ♈	1 ♑ 6 ♒	1 ♈ 10 ♉	1 ♒ 4 ♓ 28 ♈	1 ♒	1 ♈ 23 ♉	1 ♒ 18 ♓
APR	1 ♉ 21 ♈	1 ♈ 7 ♉	1 ♓ 27 ♈	1 ♉ 6 ♊	1 ♈ 21 ♉	1 ♒ 7 ♓	1 ♉ 17 ♊	1 ♓ 12 ♈
MAY	1 ♈	1 ♊ 26 ♋	1 ♈ 22 ♉	1 ♊ 7 ♋	1 ♉ 16 ♊	1 ♓ 7 ♈	1 ♊ 12 ♋	1 ♈ 6 ♉ 30 ♊
JUN	1 ♈ 4 ♉	1 ♋ 20 ♌	1 ♉ 15 ♊	1 ♋ 15 ♊	1 ♊ 9 ♋	1 ♈ 3 ♉ 29 ♊	1 ♋ 8 ♌	1 ♊ 24 ♋
JUL	1 ♉ 9 ♊	1 ♌ 15 ♍	1 ♊ 10 ♋	1 ♊ 14 ♋	1 ♋ 4 ♌ 28 ♍	1 ♊ 24 ♋	1 ♌ 8 ♍	1 ♋ 18 ♌
AUG	1 ♊ 6 ♋	1 ♍ 11 ♎	1 ♋ 4 ♌ 28 ♍	1 ♋	1 ♍ 22 ♎	1 ♋ 18 ♌	1 ♍	1 ♌ 12 ♍
SEP	1 ♌ 26 ♍	1 ♎ 8 ♏	1 ♍ 21 ♎	1 ♋ 9 ♌	1 ♎ 16 ♏	1 ♌ 12 ♍	1 ♍	1 ♍ 5 ♎ 29 ♏
OCT	1 ♍ 21 ♎	1 ♏ 13 ♐	1 ♎ 15 ♏	1 ♌ 8 ♍	1 ♏ 12 ♐	1 ♍ 6 ♎ 30 ♏	1 ♍	1 ♏ 24 ♐
NOV	1 ♎ 14 ♏	1 ♐ 23 ♏	1 ♏ 8 ♐	1 ♍ 3 ♎ 28 ♏	1 ♐ 7 ♑	1 ♏ 23 ♐	1 ♍ 10 ♎	1 ♐ 17 ♑
DEC	1 ♏ 8 ♐ 31 ♑	1 ♏	1 ♐ 2 ♑ 26 ♒	1 ♏ 22 ♐	1 ♑ 6 ♒	1 ♐ 17 ♑	1 ♎ 9 ♏	1 ♑ 12 ♒

♀	1937	1938	1939	1940	1941	1942	1943	1944
JAN	1♒ 7♓	1♑ 24♒	1♏ 5♐	1♒ 19♓	1♐ 14♑	1♒	1♑ 9♒	1♏ 4♐ 29♑
FEB	1♓ 3♈	1♒ 17♓	1♐ 7♑	1♓ 13♈	1♑ 7♒	1♒	1♒ 2♓ 26♈	1♑ 22♒
MAR	1♈ 10♉	1♓ 13♈	1♑ 6♒	1♈ 9♉	1♒ 3♓ 28♈	1♒	1♈ 22♉	1♒ 18♓
APR	1♉ 15♈	1♈ 6♉ 30♊	1♓ 26♈	1♉ 5♊	1♈ 21♉	1♒ 7♓	1♉ 16♊	1♓ 11♈
MAY	1♈	1♊ 25♋	1♈ 21♉	1♊ 21♋	1♉ 15♊	1♓ 7♈	1♊ 12♋	1♈ 5♉ 30♊
JUN	1♈ 5♉	1♋ 19♌	1♉ 15♊	1♋	1♊ 8♋	1♈ 3♉ 28♊	1♋ 8♌	1♊ 23♋
JUL	1♉ 8♊	1♌ 15♍	1♊ 10♋	1♋ 6♊	1♋ 3♌ 28♍	1♊ 24♋	1♌ 8♍	1♋ 18♌
AUG	1♊ 5♋	1♍ 10♎	1♋ 3♌ 27♍	1♊ 2♋	1♍ 22♎	1♋ 18♌	1♍	1♌ 11♍
SEP	1♌ 26♍	1♎ 8♏	1♍ 21♎	1♋ 9♌	1♎ 16♏	1♌ 11♍	1♍	1♍ 4♎ 29♏
OCT	1♍ 19♎	1♏ 14♐	1♎ 15♏	1♌ 7♍	1♏ 11♐	1♍ 5♎ 29♏	1♍	1♏ 23♐
NOV	1♎ 13♏	1♐ 16♏	1♏ 8♐	1♍ 2♎ 27♏	1♐ 7♑	1♏ 22♐	1♍ 10♎	1♐ 17♑
DEC	1♏ 7♐ 31♑	1♏	1♐ 2♑ 26♒	1♏ 21♐	1♑ 6♒	1♐ 16♑	1♎ 9♏	1♑ 12♒

♀	1945	1946	1947	1948	1949	1950	1951	1952
JAN	1♒ 6♓	1♑ 23♒	1♏ 6♐	1♒ 19♓	1♐ 14♑	1♒	1♑ 8♒	1♏ 3♐ 28♑
FEB	1♓ 3♈	1♒ 16♓	1♐ 7♑	1♓ 12♈	1♑ 7♒	1♒	1♓ 25♈	1♑ 21♒
MAR	1♈ 12♉	1♓ 12♈	1♑ 6♒ 31♓	1♈ 8♉	1♒ 3♓ 27♈	1♒	1♈ 22♉	1♒ 17♓
APR	1♉ 8♈	1♈ 6♉ 30♊	1♓ 26♈	1♉ 5♊	1♈ 20♉	1♒ 7♓	1♉ 16♊	1♓ 10♈
MAY	1♈	1♊ 25♋	1♈ 21♉	1♊ 8♋	1♉ 15♊	1♓ 7♈	1♊ 12♋	1♈ 5♉ 29♊
JUN	1♈ 5♉	1♋ 19♌	1♉ 14♊	1♋ 30♊	1♊ 8♋	1♈ 2♉ 28♊	1♋ 9♌	1♊ 23♋
JUL	1♉ 8♊	1♌ 14♍	1♊ 9♋	1♊	1♋ 2♌ 27♍	1♊ 23♋	1♌ 9♍	1♋ 17♌
AUG	1♊ 5♋ 30♌	1♍ 10♎	1♋ 3♌ 27♍	1♊ 4♋	1♍ 21♎	1♋ 17♌	1♍	1♌ 10♍
SEP	1♌ 25♍	1♎ 8♏	1♍ 20♎	1♋ 9♌	1♎ 15♏	1♌ 11♍	1♍	1♍ 4♎ 28♏
OCT	1♍ 17♎	1♏ 17♐	1♎ 14♏	1♌ 7♍	1♏ 11♐	1♍ 5♎ 29♏	1♍	1♏ 23♐
NOV	1♎ 13♏	1♐ 9♏	1♏ 7♐	1♍ 2♎ 27♏	1♐ 7♑	1♏ 22♐	1♍ 10♎	1♐ 16♑
DEC	1♏ 7♐ 31♑	1♏	1♐ 2♑ 25♒	1♏ 21♐	1♑ 7♒	1♐ 15♑	1♎ 9♏	1♑ 11♒

♀	1953	1954	1955	1956	1957	1958	1959	1960
JAN	1 ♒ 6 ♓	1 ♑ 23 ♒	1 ♏ 7 ♐	1 ♒ 18 ♓	1 ♐ 13 ♑	1 ♒	1 ♑ 8 ♒	1 ♏ 3 ♐ 28 ♑
FEB	1 ♓ 3 ♈	1 ♒ 16 ♓	1 ♐ 7 ♑	1 ♓ 12 ♈	1 ♑ 6 ♒	1 ♒	1 ♓ 25 ♈	1 ♑ 21 ♒
MAR	1 ♈ 15 ♉	1 ♓ 12 ♈	1 ♑ 5 ♒ 31 ♓	1 ♈ 8 ♉	1 ♒ 2 ♓ 26 ♈	1 ♒	1 ♈ 21 ♉	1 ♒ 16 ♓
APR	1 ♈	1 ♈ 5 ♉ 29 ♊	1 ♓ 25 ♈	1 ♉ 5 ♊	1 ♈ 19 ♉	1 ♒ 7 ♓	1 ♉ 15 ♊	1 ♓ 10 ♈
MAY	1 ♈	1 ♊ 24 ♋	1 ♈ 20 ♉	1 ♊	1 ♉ 14 ♊	1 ♈ 6 ♉	1 ♊ 11 ♋	1 ♈ 4 ♉ 29 ♊
JUN	1 ♈ 8 ♉	1 ♋ 18 ♌	1 ♉ 14 ♊	1 ♋ 24	1 ♉ 7 ♊	1 ♈ 8 ♉ 27 ♊	1 ♋ 7 ♌	1 ♊ 22 ♋
JUL	1 ♉ 8 ♊	1 ♊ 14 ♍	1 ♊ 9 ♋	1 ♊	1 ♋ 2 ♌ 27 ♍	1 ♊ 22 ♋	1 ♌ 9 ♍	1 ♋ 16 ♌
AUG	1 ♊ 5 ♋ 31 ♌	1 ♍ 10 ♎	1 ♋ 2 ♌ 26 ♍	1 ♊ 5 ♋	1 ♍ 21 ♎	1 ♋ 16 ♌	1 ♍	1 ♌ 9 ♍
SEP	1 ♌ 25 ♍	1 ♎ 7 ♏	1 ♍ 19 ♎	1 ♋ 9 ♌	1 ♎ 15 ♏	1 ♌ 10 ♍	1 ♎ 21 ♍ 26 ♏	1 ♌ 3 ♍ 28 ♎
OCT	1 ♍ 19 ♎	1 ♏ 24 ♐ 28 ♏	1 ♎ 13 ♏	1 ♌ 7 ♍	1 ♏ 11 ♐	1 ♎ 3 ♏ 28 ♎	1 ♍	1 ♏ 22 ♐
NOV	1 ♎ 12 ♏	1 ♏	1 ♏ 6 ♐	1 ♎ 26 ♏	1 ♐ 6 ♏	1 ♏ 21 ♐	1 ♍ 10 ♎	1 ♐ 16 ♏
DEC	1 ♏ 6 ♐ 30 ♑	1 ♏	1 ♑ 25 ♒	1 ♏ 20 ♐	1 ♑ 7 ♒	1 ♐ 15 ♑	1 ♎ 8 ♏	1 ♑ 11 ♒

♀	1961	1962	1963	1964	1965	1966	1967	1968
JAN	1 ♒ 6 ♓	1 ♑ 22 ♒	1 ♏ 7 ♐	1 ♒ 17 ♓	1 ♐ 13 ♑	1 ♒	1 ♑ 7 ♒ 31 ♓	1 ♏ 2 ♐ 27 ♑
FEB	1 ♓ 3 ♈	1 ♒ 15 ♓	1 ♐ 6 ♑	1 ♓ 11 ♈	1 ♑ 6 ♒	1 ♓ 7 ♒ 26 ♓	1 ♓ 24 ♈	1 ♑ 21 ♒
MAR	1 ♈	1 ♓ 11 ♈	1 ♑ 5 ♒ 31 ♓	1 ♈ 8 ♉	1 ♒ 2 ♓ 26 ♈	1 ♒	1 ♈ 21 ♉	1 ♒ 16 ♓
APR	1 ♈	1 ♈ 4 ♉ 29 ♊	1 ♓ 25 ♈	1 ♉ 5 ♊	1 ♈ 19 ♉	1 ♒ 7 ♓	1 ♉ 15 ♊	1 ♓ 9 ♈
MAY	1 ♈	1 ♊ 24 ♋	1 ♈ 19 ♉	1 ♊ 10	1 ♉ 13 ♊	1 ♈ 6 ♉	1 ♊ 11 ♋	1 ♈ 4 ♉ 28 ♊
JUN	1 ♈ 6 ♉	1 ♋ 18 ♌	1 ♉ 13 ♊	1 ♊ 18 ♋	1 ♉ 7 ♊	1 ♉ 8 ♊	1 ♋ 7 ♌	1 ♊ 21 ♋
JUL	1 ♉ 8 ♊	1 ♊ 13 ♋	1 ♊ 8 ♋	1 ♊	1 ♋ 26 ♍	1 ♋ 22 ♋	1 ♌ 9 ♍	1 ♋ 16 ♌
AUG	1 ♊ 4 ♋ 30 ♌	1 ♍ 9 ♎	1 ♌ 26 ♍	1 ♊ 6 ♋	1 ♍ 20 ♎	1 ♋ 16 ♌	1 ♍	1 ♌ 9 ♍
SEP	1 ♌ 24 ♍	1 ♎ 8 ♏	1 ♍ 18 ♎	1 ♋ 9 ♌	1 ♎ 14 ♏	1 ♌ 9 ♍	1 ♍ 10 ♎	1 ♌ 3 ♍ 27 ♎
OCT	1 ♍ 18 ♎	1 ♏	1 ♎ 13 ♏	1 ♌ 6 ♍	1 ♏ 10 ♐	1 ♍ 3 ♎ 27 ♏	1 ♌ 2 ♍	1 ♏ 22 ♐
NOV	1 ♎ 12 ♏	1 ♏	1 ♏ 6 ♐ 30 ♑	1 ♎ 25 ♏	1 ♐ 6 ♏	1 ♏ 20 ♐	1 ♍ 10 ♎	1 ♐ 15 ♏
DEC	1 ♏ 6 ♐ 29 ♑	1 ♏	1 ♑ 24 ♒	1 ♏ 20 ♐	1 ♑ 8 ♒	1 ♐ 14 ♑	1 ♎ 8 ♏	1 ♑ 10 ♒

– VENUS TABLES –

♀	1969	1970	1971	1972	1973	1974	1975	1976
JAN	1 ♒, 5 ♓	1 ♑, 22 ♒	1 ♏, 8 ♐	1 ♒, 17 ♓	1 ♐, 12 ♑	1 ♒, 30 ♑	1 ♑, 7 ♒, 31 ♓	1 ♏, 2 ♐, 27 ♑
FEB	1 ♓, 3 ♈	1 ♒, 15 ♓	1 ♐, 6 ♑	1 ♓, 11 ♈	1 ♑, 5 ♒	1 ♑	1 ♓, 24 ♈	1 ♑, 20 ♒
MAR	1 ♈	1 ♓, 11 ♈	1 ♑, 5 ♒, 30 ♓	1 ♈, 8 ♉	1 ♓, 25 ♈	1 ♒	1 ♈, 20 ♉	1 ♒, 15 ♓
APR	1 ♈	1 ♈, 4 ♉, 28 ♊	1 ♓, 24 ♈	1 ♉, 4 ♊	1 ♈, 19 ♉	1 ♒, 7 ♓	1 ♉, 14 ♊	1 ♓, 9 ♈
MAY	1 ♈	1 ♊, 23 ♋	1 ♈, 19 ♉	1 ♊, 11 ♋	1 ♉, 13 ♊	1 ♓, 5 ♈	1 ♊, 10 ♋	1 ♈, 3 ♉, 27 ♊
JUN	1 ♈, 6 ♉	1 ♋, 17 ♌	1 ♉, 13 ♊	1 ♋, 12 ♊	1 ♊, 6 ♋	1 ♉, 26 ♊	1 ♋, 7 ♌	1 ♊, 21 ♋
JUL	1 ♉, 7 ♊	1 ♌, 13 ♍	1 ♊, 7 ♋, 31 ♌	1 ♊	1 ♌, 26 ♍	1 ♊, 22 ♋	1 ♌, 10 ♍	1 ♋, 15 ♌
AUG	1 ♊, 4 ♋, 30 ♌	1 ♍, 9 ♎	1 ♌, 25 ♍	1 ♊, 8 ♋	1 ♍, 19 ♎	1 ♋, 15 ♌	1 ♍	1 ♌, 9 ♍
SEP	1 ♌, 24 ♍	1 ♎, 8 ♏	1 ♍, 18 ♎	1 ♋, 8 ♌	1 ♎, 14 ♏	1 ♌, 9 ♍	1 ♍, 3 ♌	1 ♍, 2 ♎, 26 ♏
OCT	1 ♍, 18 ♎	1 ♏	1 ♎, 12 ♏	1 ♌, 6 ♍, 31 ♎	1 ♏, 10 ♐	1 ♍, 3 ♎, 27 ♏	1 ♌, 5 ♍	1 ♏, 21 ♐
NOV	1 ♎, 11 ♏	1 ♏	1 ♏, 5 ♐, 30 ♑	1 ♎, 25 ♏	1 ♐, 6 ♑	1 ♏, 20 ♐	1 ♍, 10 ♎	1 ♐, 15 ♑
DEC	1 ♏, 5 ♐, 29 ♑	1 ♏	1 ♑, 24 ♒	1 ♏, 19 ♐	1 ♑, 8 ♒	1 ♐, 14 ♑	1 ♎, 7 ♏	1 ♑, 10 ♒

♀	1977	1978	1979	1980	1981	1982	1983	1984
JAN	1 ♒, 5 ♓	1 ♑, 21 ♒	1 ♏, 8 ♐	1 ♒, 16 ♓	1 ♐, 12 ♑	1 ♒, 24 ♑	1 ♑, 6 ♒, 30 ♓	1 ♏, 2 ♐, 26 ♑
FEB	1 ♓, 3 ♈	1 ♒, 14 ♓	1 ♐, 6 ♑	1 ♓, 10 ♈	1 ♑, 5 ♒, 28 ♓	1 ♑	1 ♓, 23 ♈	1 ♑, 20 ♒
MAR	1 ♈	1 ♓, 10 ♈	1 ♑, 4 ♒, 29 ♓	1 ♈, 7 ♉	1 ♓, 25 ♈	1 ♑, 3 ♒	1 ♈, 20 ♉	1 ♒, 15 ♓
APR	1 ♈	1 ♈, 3 ♉, 28 ♊	1 ♓, 23 ♈	1 ♉, 4 ♊	1 ♈, 18 ♉	1 ♒, 7 ♓	1 ♉, 14 ♊	1 ♓, 8 ♈
MAY	1 ♈	1 ♊, 22 ♋	1 ♈, 18 ♉	1 ♊, 13 ♋	1 ♉, 12 ♊	1 ♓, 5 ♈, 31 ♉	1 ♊, 10 ♋	1 ♈, 3 ♉, 27 ♊
JUN	1 ♈, 7 ♉	1 ♋, 17 ♌	1 ♉, 12 ♊	1 ♋, 6 ♊	1 ♊, 6 ♋, 30 ♌	1 ♉, 26 ♊	1 ♋, 7 ♌	1 ♊, 21 ♋
JUL	1 ♉, 7 ♊	1 ♌, 12 ♍	1 ♊, 7 ♋, 31 ♌	1 ♊	1 ♌, 25 ♍	1 ♊, 21 ♋	1 ♌, 11 ♍	1 ♋, 15 ♌
AUG	1 ♊, 3 ♋, 29 ♌	1 ♍, 8 ♎	1 ♌, 25 ♍	1 ♊, 6 ♋	1 ♍, 19 ♎	1 ♋, 15 ♌	1 ♍, 28 ♌	1 ♌, 8 ♍
SEP	1 ♌, 23 ♍	1 ♎, 8 ♏	1 ♍, 18 ♎	1 ♋, 8 ♌	1 ♎, 13 ♏	1 ♌, 8 ♍	1 ♌	1 ♍, 2 ♎, 26 ♏
OCT	1 ♍, 17 ♎	1 ♏	1 ♎, 12 ♏	1 ♌, 5 ♍, 31 ♎	1 ♏, 9 ♐	1 ♍, 2 ♎, 26 ♏	1 ♌, 6 ♍	1 ♏, 21 ♐
NOV	1 ♎, 11 ♏	1 ♏	1 ♏, 5 ♐, 29 ♑	1 ♎, 25 ♏	1 ♐, 6 ♑	1 ♏, 19 ♐	1 ♍, 10 ♎	1 ♐, 14 ♑
DEC	1 ♏, 4 ♐, 28 ♑	1 ♏	1 ♑, 23 ♒	1 ♏, 19 ♐	1 ♑, 9 ♒	1 ♐, 12 ♑	1 ♎, 7 ♏	1 ♑, 10 ♒

♀	1985	1986	1987	1988	1989	1990	1991	1992
JAN	1 ♒ 5 ♓	1 ♑ 21 ♒	1 ♏ 8 ♐	1 ♒ 16 ♓	1 ♐ 11 ♑	1 ♒ 17 ♑	1 ♑ 6 ♒ 30 ♓	1 ♐ 26 ♑
FEB	1 ♓ 3 ♈	1 ♒ 14 ♓	1 ♐ 6 ♑	1 ♓ 10 ♈	1 ♑ 4 ♒ 28 ♓	1 ♑	1 ♓ 23 ♈	1 ♑ 19 ♒
MAR	1 ♈	1 ♓ 9 ♈	1 ♑ 4 ♒ 29 ♓	1 ♈ 7 ♉	1 ♓ 24 ♈	1 ♑ 4 ♒	1 ♈ 19 ♉	1 ♒ 14 ♓
APR	1 ♈	1 ♈ 3 ♉ 27 ♊	1 ♓ 23 ♈	1 ♉ 4 ♊	1 ♈ 17 ♉	1 ♒ 7 ♓	1 ♉ 13 ♊	1 ♓ 7 ♈
MAY	1 ♈	1 ♊ 22 ♋	1 ♈ 18 ♉	1 ♊ 18 ♋ 27 ♊	1 ♉ 12 ♊	1 ♓ 4 ♈ 31 ♉	1 ♊ 9 ♋	1 ♈ 2 ♉ 26 ♊
JUN	1 ♈ 7 ♉	1 ♋ 16 ♌	1 ♉ 12 ♊	1 ♊	1 ♊ 5 ♋ 30 ♌	1 ♉ 25 ♊	1 ♋ 7 ♌	1 ♊ 20 ♋
JUL	1 ♉ 7 ♊	1 ♌ 12 ♍	1 ♊ 6 ♋ 31 ♌	1 ♊	1 ♌ 24 ♍	1 ♊ 20 ♋	1 ♌ 11 ♍	1 ♋ 14 ♌
AUG	1 ♊ 3 ♋ 28 ♌	1 ♍ 8 ♎	1 ♌ 24 ♍	1 ♊ 7 ♋	1 ♍ 18 ♎	1 ♋ 13 ♌	1 ♍ 22 ♌	1 ♌ 7 ♍
SEP	1 ♌ 23 ♍	1 ♎ 8 ♏	1 ♍ 17 ♎	1 ♋ 8 ♌	1 ♎ 13 ♏	1 ♌ 9 ♍	1 ♌	1 ♍ 25 ♎
OCT	1 ♍ 17 ♎	1 ♏	1 ♎ 11 ♏	1 ♌ 5 ♍ 30 ♎	1 ♏ 9 ♐	1 ♍ 2 ♎ 26 ♏	1 ♌ 7 ♍	1 ♎ 20 ♏
NOV	1 ♎ 10 ♏	1 ♏	1 ♏ 4 ♐ 28 ♑	1 ♎ 24 ♏	1 ♐ 6 ♑	1 ♏ 19 ♐	1 ♍ 9 ♎	1 ♏ 14 ♐
DEC	1 ♏ 4 ♐ 28 ♑	1 ♏	1 ♑ 23 ♒	1 ♏ 18 ♐	1 ♑ 10 ♒	1 ♐ 13 ♑	1 ♎ 7 ♏	1 ♐ 9 ♑

♀	1993	1994	1995	1996	1997	1998	1999	2000
JAN	1 ♒ 4 ♓	1 ♑ 20 ♒	1 ♏ 8 ♐	1 ♒ 15 ♓	1 ♐ 10 ♑	1 ♒ 10 ♑	1 ♑ 5 ♒ 29 ♓	1 ♐ 25 ♑
FEB	1 ♓ 3 ♈	1 ♒ 13 ♓	1 ♐ 5 ♑	1 ♓ 9 ♈	1 ♑ 4 ♒ 28 ♓	1 ♑	1 ♓ 22 ♈	1 ♑ 19 ♒
MAR	1 ♈	1 ♓ 9 ♈	1 ♑ 3 ♒ 29 ♓	1 ♈ 6 ♉	1 ♓ 24 ♈	1 ♑ 5 ♒	1 ♈ 19 ♉	1 ♒ 14 ♓
APR	1 ♈	1 ♈ 2 ♉ 27 ♊	1 ♓ 23 ♈	1 ♉ 4 ♊	1 ♈ 17 ♉	1 ♒ 7 ♓	1 ♉ 13 ♊	1 ♓ 7 ♈
MAY	1 ♈	1 ♊ 21 ♋	1 ♈ 17 ♉	1 ♊	1 ♉ 11 ♊	1 ♓ 4 ♈ 30 ♉	1 ♊ 9 ♋	1 ♈ 2 ♉ 26 ♊
JUN	1 ♈ 7 ♉	1 ♋ 15 ♌	1 ♉ 11 ♊	1 ♊	1 ♊ 4 ♋ 29 ♌	1 ♉ 25 ♊	1 ♋ 6 ♌	1 ♊ 19 ♋
JUL	1 ♉ 6 ♊	1 ♌ 12 ♍	1 ♊ 6 ♋ 30 ♌	1 ♊	1 ♌ 24 ♍	1 ♊ 20 ♋	1 ♌ 13 ♍	1 ♋ 14 ♌
AUG	1 ♊ 2 ♋ 28 ♌	1 ♍ 8 ♎	1 ♌ 23 ♍	1 ♊ 8 ♋	1 ♍ 18 ♎	1 ♋ 14 ♌	1 ♍ 16 ♌	1 ♌ 7 ♍
SEP	1 ♌ 22 ♍	1 ♎ 8 ♏	1 ♍ 17 ♎	1 ♋ 7 ♌	1 ♎ 12 ♏	1 ♌ 7 ♍	1 ♌	1 ♍ 25 ♎
OCT	1 ♍ 16 ♎	1 ♏	1 ♎ 10 ♏	1 ♌ 4 ♍ 29 ♎	1 ♏ 9 ♐	1 ♎ 25 ♏	1 ♌ 8 ♍	1 ♎ 20 ♏
NOV	1 ♎ 9 ♏	1 ♏	1 ♏ 3 ♐ 27 ♑	1 ♎ 23 ♏	1 ♐ 6 ♑	1 ♏ 18 ♐	1 ♍ 10 ♎	1 ♏ 13 ♐
DEC	1 ♏ 3 ♐ 27 ♑	1 ♏	1 ♑ 22 ♒	1 ♏ 17 ♐	1 ♑ 12 ♒	1 ♐ 12 ♑	1 ♎ 6 ♏	1 ♐ 9 ♑

♂	1921	1922	1923	1924	1925	1926	1927	1928	1929	1930
JAN	1 ♒, 5 ♓	1 ♏	1 ♓, 21 ♈	1 ♏, 19 ♐	1 ♈	1 ♐	1 ♉	1 ♐, 19 ♑	1 ♊	1 ♑
FEB	1 ♓, 13 ♈	1 ♏, 18 ♐	1 ♈	1 ♐	1 ♈, 5 ♉	1 ♐, 9 ♑	1 ♉, 22 ♊	1 ♑, 28 ♒	1 ♊	1 ♑, 6 ♒
MAR	1 ♈, 25 ♉	1 ♐	1 ♈, 4 ♉	1 ♐, 6 ♑	1 ♉, 24 ♊	1 ♑, 23 ♒	1 ♊	1 ♒	1 ♊, 10 ♋	1 ♒, 17 ♓
APR	1 ♉	1 ♐	1 ♉, 16 ♊	1 ♑, 24 ♒	1 ♊	1 ♒	1 ♊, 17 ♋	1 ♒, 7 ♓	1 ♋	1 ♓, 24 ♈
MAY	1 ♉, 6 ♊	1 ♐	1 ♊, 30 ♋	1 ♒	1 ♊, 9 ♋	1 ♒, 3 ♓	1 ♋	1 ♓, 16 ♈	1 ♋, 13 ♌	1 ♈
JUN	1 ♊, 18 ♋	1 ♐	1 ♋	1 ♒, 24 ♓	1 ♋, 26 ♌	1 ♓, 15 ♈	1 ♋, 6 ♌	1 ♈, 26 ♉	1 ♌	1 ♈, 3 ♉
JUL	1 ♋	1 ♐	1 ♋, 16 ♌	1 ♓	1 ♌	1 ♈	1 ♌, 25 ♍	1 ♉	1 ♌, 4 ♍	1 ♉, 14 ♊
AUG	1 ♋, 3 ♌	1 ♐	1 ♌	1 ♓, 24 ♒	1 ♌, 12 ♍	1 ♉	1 ♍	1 ♉, 9 ♊	1 ♍, 21 ♎	1 ♊, 28 ♋
SEP	1 ♌, 19 ♍	1 ♐, 13 ♑	1 ♍	1 ♒	1 ♍, 28 ♎	1 ♉	1 ♍, 10 ♎	1 ♊	1 ♎	1 ♋
OCT	1 ♍	1 ♑, 30 ♒	1 ♍, 18 ♎	1 ♒, 19 ♓	1 ♎	1 ♉	1 ♎, 26 ♏	1 ♊, 3 ♋	1 ♎, 6 ♏	1 ♋, 20 ♌
NOV	1 ♍, 6 ♎	1 ♒	1 ♎	1 ♓	1 ♎, 13 ♏	1 ♉	1 ♏	1 ♋	1 ♏, 18 ♐	1 ♌
DEC	1 ♎, 26 ♏	1 ♒, 11 ♓	1 ♎, 4 ♏	1 ♓, 19 ♈	1 ♏, 28 ♐	1 ♉	1 ♏, 8 ♐	1 ♋, 20 ♊	1 ♐, 29 ♑	1 ♌

♂	1931	1932	1933	1934	1935	1936	1937	1938	1939	1940
JAN	1 ♌	1 ♑, 18 ♒	1 ♍	1 ♒	1 ♎	1 ♒, 14 ♓	1 ♎, 5 ♏	1 ♓, 30 ♈	1 ♏, 29 ♐	1 ♓, 4 ♈
FEB	1 ♌, 16 ♋	1 ♒, 25 ♓	1 ♍	1 ♒, 4 ♓	1 ♎	1 ♓, 22 ♈	1 ♏	1 ♈	1 ♐	1 ♈, 17 ♉
MAR	1 ♋, 30 ♌	1 ♓	1 ♍	1 ♓, 14 ♈	1 ♎	1 ♈	1 ♏, 13 ♐	1 ♈, 12 ♉	1 ♐, 21 ♑	1 ♉
APR	1 ♌	1 ♓, 3 ♈	1 ♍	1 ♈, 22 ♉	1 ♎	1 ♉	1 ♐	1 ♉, 23 ♊	1 ♑	1 ♊
MAY	1 ♌	1 ♈, 12 ♉	1 ♍	1 ♉	1 ♎	1 ♉, 13 ♊	1 ♐, 14 ♏	1 ♊	1 ♑, 25 ♒	1 ♊, 17 ♋
JUN	1 ♌, 10 ♍	1 ♉, 8 ♊	1 ♍	1 ♉, 2 ♊	1 ♎	1 ♊, 25 ♋	1 ♏	1 ♊, 7 ♋	1 ♒	1 ♋
JUL	1 ♍	1 ♊	1 ♍, 6 ♎	1 ♊, 15 ♋	1 ♎, 29 ♏	1 ♋	1 ♏	1 ♋, 22 ♌	1 ♒, 21 ♑	1 ♋, 3 ♌
AUG	1 ♎	1 ♊, 4 ♋	1 ♎, 26 ♏	1 ♋, 30 ♌	1 ♏	1 ♋, 10 ♌	1 ♏, 8 ♐	1 ♌	1 ♑	1 ♌, 19 ♍
SEP	1 ♎, 17 ♏	1 ♋, 20 ♌	1 ♏	1 ♌	1 ♏, 16 ♐	1 ♌, 26 ♍	1 ♐, 30 ♑	1 ♌, 7 ♍	1 ♑, 24 ♒	1 ♍
OCT	1 ♏, 30 ♐	1 ♌	1 ♏, 9 ♐	1 ♌, 18 ♍	1 ♐, 28 ♑	1 ♍	1 ♑	1 ♍, 25 ♎	1 ♒	1 ♍, 5 ♎
NOV	1 ♐	1 ♌, 13 ♍	1 ♐, 19 ♑	1 ♍	1 ♑	1 ♍, 14 ♎	1 ♑, 11 ♒	1 ♎	1 ♒, 19 ♓	1 ♎, 20 ♏
DEC	1 ♐, 10 ♑	1 ♍	1 ♑, 28 ♒	1 ♍, 11 ♎	1 ♑, 7 ♒	1 ♎	1 ♒, 21 ♓	1 ♎, 11 ♏	1 ♓	1 ♏

♂	1941	1942	1943	1944	1945	1946	1947	1948	1949	1950
JAN	1 ♏ / 4 ♐	1 ♈ / 11 ♉	1 ♐ / 26 ♑	1 ♊	1 ♐ / 5 ♑	1 ♋	1 ♑ / 25 ♒	1 ♍	1 ♑ / 4 ♒	1 ♎
FEB	1 ♐ / 17 ♑	1 ♉	1 ♑	1 ♊	1 ♑ / 14 ♒	1 ♋	1 ♒	1 ♍ / 12 ♌	1 ♒ / 11 ♓	1 ♎
MAR	1 ♑	1 ♉ / 7 ♊	1 ♑ / 8 ♒	1 ♊ / 29 ♋	1 ♒ / 25 ♓	1 ♋	1 ♒ / 4 ♓	1 ♌	1 ♓ / 21 ♈	1 ♎ / 28 ♍
APR	1 ♑ / 2 ♒	1 ♊ / 26 ♋	1 ♒ / 17 ♓	1 ♋	1 ♓	1 ♋ / 22 ♌	1 ♓ / 11 ♈	1 ♌	1 ♈ / 30 ♉	1 ♍
MAY	1 ♒ / 16 ♓	1 ♋	1 ♓ / 27 ♈	1 ♋ / 22 ♌	1 ♓ / 3 ♈	1 ♌	1 ♈ / 21 ♉	1 ♌ / 18 ♍	1 ♉	1 ♍
JUN	1 ♓	1 ♋ / 14 ♌	1 ♈	1 ♌	1 ♈ / 11 ♉	1 ♌ / 20 ♍	1 ♉	1 ♍	1 ♉ / 10 ♊	1 ♍ / 11 ♎
JUL	1 ♓ / 2 ♈	1 ♌	1 ♈ / 7 ♉	1 ♌ / 12 ♍	1 ♉ / 23 ♊	1 ♍	1 ♊	1 ♍ / 17 ♎	1 ♊ / 23 ♋	1 ♎
AUG	1 ♈	1 ♍	1 ♉ / 23 ♊	1 ♍ / 29 ♎	1 ♊	1 ♍ / 9 ♎	1 ♊ / 13 ♋	1 ♎	1 ♋	1 ♎ / 10 ♏
SEP	1 ♈	1 ♍ / 17 ♎	1 ♊	1 ♎	1 ♊ / 7 ♋	1 ♎ / 24 ♏	1 ♋	1 ♎ / 3 ♏	1 ♋ / 7 ♌	1 ♏ / 25 ♐
OCT	1 ♈	1 ♎	1 ♊	1 ♎ / 13 ♏	1 ♋	1 ♏	1 ♌	1 ♏ / 17 ♐	1 ♌ / 27 ♍	1 ♐
NOV	1 ♈	1 ♎ / 2 ♏	1 ♊	1 ♏ / 25 ♐	1 ♋ / 11 ♌	1 ♏ / 6 ♐	1 ♌	1 ♐ / 26 ♑	1 ♍	1 ♐ / 6 ♑
DEC	1 ♈	1 ♏ / 15 ♐	1 ♊	1 ♐	1 ♌ / 26 ♋	1 ♐ / 17 ♑	1 ♍	1 ♑	1 ♍ / 26 ♎	1 ♑ / 15 ♒

♂	1951	1952	1953	1954	1955	1956	1957	1958	1959	1960
JAN	1 ♒ / 22 ♓	1 ♎ / 20 ♏	1 ♓	1 ♏	1 ♓ / 15 ♈	1 ♏ / 14 ♐	1 ♈ / 28 ♉	1 ♐	1 ♉	1 ♐ / 14 ♑
FEB	1 ♓	1 ♏	1 ♓ / 8 ♈	1 ♏ / 9 ♐	1 ♈ / 26 ♉	1 ♐ / 28 ♑	1 ♉	1 ♐ / 3 ♑	1 ♉ / 10 ♊	1 ♑ / 23 ♒
MAR	1 ♓ / 2 ♈	1 ♏	1 ♈ / 20 ♉	1 ♐	1 ♉	1 ♑	1 ♉ / 17 ♊	1 ♑ / 17 ♒	1 ♊	1 ♒
APR	1 ♈ / 10 ♉	1 ♏	1 ♉	1 ♐ / 12 ♑	1 ♉ / 10 ♊	1 ♑ / 14 ♒	1 ♊	1 ♒ / 27 ♓	1 ♊ / 10 ♋	1 ♒ / 2 ♓
MAY	1 ♉ / 21 ♊	1 ♏	1 ♊	1 ♑	1 ♊ / 26 ♋	1 ♒	1 ♊ / 4 ♋	1 ♓	1 ♋	1 ♓ / 11 ♈
JUN	1 ♊	1 ♏	1 ♊ / 14 ♋	1 ♑	1 ♋	1 ♒ / 3 ♓	1 ♋ / 21 ♌	1 ♓ / 7 ♈	1 ♋ / 2 ♌	1 ♈ / 20 ♉
JUL	1 ♊ / 3 ♋	1 ♏	1 ♋ / 29 ♌	1 ♑ / 3 ♒	1 ♋ / 11 ♌	1 ♋ / 2 ♌	1 ♌	1 ♈ / 21 ♉	1 ♌ / 20 ♍	1 ♉
AUG	1 ♋ / 18 ♌	1 ♏ / 27 ♐	1 ♌	1 ♐ / 24 ♑	1 ♌ / 27 ♍	1 ♋	1 ♌ / 8 ♍	1 ♉	1 ♍	1 ♉ / 2 ♊
SEP	1 ♌	1 ♐	1 ♌ / 14 ♍	1 ♑	1 ♍	1 ♋	1 ♍ / 24 ♎	1 ♉ / 21 ♊	1 ♍ / 5 ♎	1 ♊ / 21 ♋
OCT	1 ♌ / 5 ♍	1 ♐ / 12 ♑	1 ♍	1 ♑ / 21 ♒	1 ♍ / 13 ♎	1 ♋	1 ♎	1 ♊ / 29 ♉	1 ♎ / 21 ♏	1 ♋
NOV	1 ♍ / 24 ♎	1 ♑ / 22 ♒	1 ♎	1 ♒	1 ♎ / 29 ♏	1 ♋	1 ♎ / 8 ♏	1 ♉	1 ♏	1 ♋
DEC	1 ♎	1 ♒ / 30 ♓	1 ♎ / 20 ♏	1 ♒ / 4 ♓	1 ♏	1 ♋ / 6 ♌	1 ♏ / 23 ♐	1 ♉	1 ♏ / 3 ♐	1 ♋

– MARS TABLES –

♂	1961	1962	1963	1964	1965	1966	1967	1968	1969	1970
JAN	1 ♋	1 ♑	1 ♌	1 ♑ 13 ♒	1 ♍	1 ♒ 30 ♓	1 ♎	1 ♒ 9 ♓	1 ♏	1 ♓ 24 ♈
FEB	1 ♋ 5 ♊ 7 ♋	1 ♑ 2 ♒	1 ♌	1 ♒ 20 ♓	1 ♍	1 ♓	1 ♎ 12 ♏	1 ♓ 17 ♈	1 ♏ 25 ♐	1 ♈
MAR	1 ♋	1 ♒ 12 ♓	1 ♌	1 ♓ 29 ♈	1 ♍	1 ♓ 9 ♈	1 ♏ 31 ♎	1 ♈ 28 ♉	1 ♐	1 ♈ 7 ♉
APR	1 ♋	1 ♓ 19 ♈	1 ♌	1 ♈	1 ♍	1 ♈ 17 ♉	1 ♎	1 ♉	1 ♐	1 ♉ 18 ♊
MAY	1 ♋ 6 ♌	1 ♈ 28 ♉	1 ♌	1 ♈ 7 ♉	1 ♍	1 ♉ 28 ♊	1 ♎	1 ♉ 8 ♊	1 ♐	1 ♊
JUN	1 ♌ 28 ♍	1 ♉	1 ♌ 3 ♍	1 ♉ 17 ♊	1 ♍ 29 ♎	1 ♊	1 ♎	1 ♊ 21 ♋	1 ♐	1 ♊ 2 ♋
JUL	1 ♍	1 ♉ 9 ♊	1 ♍ 27 ♎	1 ♊ 30 ♋	1 ♎	1 ♊ 11 ♋	1 ♎ 19 ♏	1 ♋	1 ♐	1 ♋ 18 ♌
AUG	1 ♍ 17 ♎	1 ♊ 22 ♋	1 ♎	1 ♋	1 ♎ 20 ♏	1 ♋ 25 ♌	1 ♏	1 ♋ 5 ♌	1 ♐	1 ♌
SEP	1 ♎	1 ♋	1 ♎ 12 ♏	1 ♋ 15 ♌	1 ♏	1 ♌	1 ♏ 10 ♐	1 ♌ 21 ♍	1 ♐ 21 ♑	1 ♌ 3 ♍
OCT	1 ♎ 2 ♏	1 ♋ 11 ♌	1 ♏ 25 ♐	1 ♌	1 ♏ 4 ♐	1 ♌ 12 ♍	1 ♐ 23 ♑	1 ♍	1 ♑	1 ♍ 20 ♎
NOV	1 ♏ 13 ♐	1 ♌	1 ♐	1 ♌ 6 ♍	1 ♐ 14 ♑	1 ♍	1 ♑	1 ♍ 9 ♎	1 ♑ 4 ♒	1 ♎
DEC	1 ♐ 24 ♑	1 ♌	1 ♐ 5 ♑	1 ♍	1 ♑ 23 ♒	1 ♍ 4 ♎	1 ♑ 2 ♒	1 ♎ 30 ♏	1 ♒ 15 ♓	1 ♎ 6 ♏

♂	1971	1972	1973	1974	1975	1976	1977	1978	1979	1980
JAN	1 ♏ 23 ♐	1 ♈	1 ♐	1 ♉	1 ♐ 21 ♑	1 ♊	1 ♑	1 ♌ 26 ♋	1 ♑ 21 ♒	1 ♍
FEB	1 ♐	1 ♈ 10 ♉	1 ♐ 12 ♑	1 ♉ 27 ♊	1 ♑	1 ♊	1 ♑ 9 ♒	1 ♋	1 ♒ 28 ♓	1 ♍
MAR	1 ♐ 12 ♑	1 ♉ 27 ♊	1 ♑ 27 ♒	1 ♊	1 ♑ 3 ♒	1 ♊ 18 ♋	1 ♒ 20 ♓	1 ♋	1 ♓	1 ♍ 12 ♌
APR	1 ♑	1 ♊	1 ♒	1 ♊ 20 ♋	1 ♒ 11 ♓	1 ♋	1 ♓ 28 ♈	1 ♋ 11 ♌	1 ♓ 7 ♈	1 ♌
MAY	1 ♑ 3 ♒	1 ♊ 12 ♋	1 ♒ 8 ♓	1 ♋	1 ♓ 21 ♈	1 ♋ 16 ♌	1 ♈	1 ♌	1 ♈ 8 ♉	1 ♌ 4 ♍
JUN	1 ♒	1 ♋ 28 ♌	1 ♓ 21 ♈	1 ♋ 9 ♌	1 ♈	1 ♌	1 ♈ 6 ♉	1 ♌ 14 ♍	1 ♉ 26 ♊	1 ♍
JUL	1 ♒	1 ♌	1 ♈	1 ♌ 27 ♍	1 ♉	1 ♌ 7 ♍	1 ♉ 18 ♊	1 ♍	1 ♊	1 ♍ 11 ♎
AUG	1 ♒	1 ♌ 15 ♍	1 ♈ 12 ♉	1 ♍	1 ♉ 14 ♊	1 ♍ 24 ♎	1 ♊	1 ♍ 4 ♎	1 ♊ 8 ♋	1 ♎ 29 ♏
SEP	1 ♒	1 ♍	1 ♉	1 ♍ 12 ♎	1 ♊	1 ♎	1 ♋	1 ♎ 20 ♏	1 ♋ 25 ♌	1 ♏
OCT	1 ♒	1 ♎	1 ♉ 30 ♈	1 ♎ 28 ♏	1 ♊ 17 ♋	1 ♎ 9 ♏	1 ♋ 27 ♌	1 ♏	1 ♌	1 ♏ 12 ♐
NOV	1 ♒ 6 ♓	1 ♎ 15 ♏	1 ♈	1 ♏	1 ♋ 26 ♊	1 ♏ 21 ♐	1 ♌	1 ♏ 2 ♐	1 ♌ 20 ♍	1 ♐ 22 ♑
DEC	1 ♓ 26 ♈	1 ♏ 15 ♐	1 ♈ 24 ♉	1 ♏ 11 ♐	1 ♊	1 ♐	1 ♌	1 ♐ 13 ♑	1 ♍	1 ♑ 31 ♒

♂	1981	1982	1983	1984	1985	1986	1987	1988	1989	1990
JAN	1 ♒	1 ♎	1 ♒ · 17 ♓	1 ♎ · 11 ♏	1 ♓	1 ♏	1 ♓ · 8 ♈	1 ♏ · 9 ♐	1 ♈ · 19 ♉	1 ♐ · 30 ♑
FEB	1 ♒ · 7 ♓	1 ♎	1 ♓ · 25 ♈	1 ♏	1 ♓ · 3 ♈	1 ♏ · 2 ♐	1 ♈ · 21 ♉	1 ♐ · 22 ♑	1 ♉	1 ♑
MAR	1 ♓ · 17 ♈	1 ♎	1 ♈	1 ♏	1 ♈ · 15 ♉	1 ♐ · 28 ♑	1 ♉	1 ♑	1 ♉ · 11 ♊	1 ♑ · 12 ♒
APR	1 ♈ · 25 ♉	1 ♎	1 ♈ · 5 ♉	1 ♏	1 ♉ · 26 ♊	1 ♑	1 ♉ · 6 ♊	1 ♑ · 7 ♒	1 ♊ · 29 ♋	1 ♒ · 21 ♓
MAY	1 ♉	1 ♎	1 ♉ · 17 ♊	1 ♏	1 ♊	1 ♑	1 ♊ · 21 ♋	1 ♒ · 22 ♓	1 ♋	1 ♓ · 31 ♈
JUN	1 ♉ · 5 ♊	1 ♎	1 ♊ · 29 ♋	1 ♏	1 ♊ · 9 ♋	1 ♑	1 ♋	1 ♓	1 ♋ · 17 ♌	1 ♈
JUL	1 ♊ · 18 ♋	1 ♎	1 ♋	1 ♏	1 ♋ · 25 ♌	1 ♑	1 ♋ · 7 ♌	1 ♓ · 14 ♈	1 ♌	1 ♈ · 13 ♉
AUG	1 ♋	1 ♎ · 3 ♏	1 ♋ · 14 ♌	1 ♏ · 18 ♐	1 ♌	1 ♑	1 ♌ · 23 ♍	1 ♈	1 ♌ · 3 ♍	1 ♉ · 31 ♊
SEP	1 ♋ · 2 ♌	1 ♏ · 20 ♐	1 ♌ · 30 ♍	1 ♐	1 ♌ · 10 ♍	1 ♑	1 ♍	1 ♈	1 ♍ · 20 ♎	1 ♊
OCT	1 ♌ · 21 ♍	1 ♐	1 ♍	1 ♐ · 5 ♑	1 ♍ · 28 ♎	1 ♑ · 9 ♒	1 ♍ · 9 ♎	1 ♈ · 24 ♓	1 ♎	1 ♊
NOV	1 ♍	1 ♑	1 ♍ · 18 ♎	1 ♑ · 16 ♒	1 ♎	1 ♒ · 26 ♓	1 ♎ · 24 ♏	1 ♓ · 2 ♈	1 ♎ · 4 ♏	1 ♊
DEC	1 ♍ · 16 ♎	1 ♑ · 10 ♒	1 ♎	1 ♒ · 25 ♓	1 ♎ · 15 ♏	1 ♓	1 ♏	1 ♈	1 ♏ · 18 ♐	1 ♊ · 14 ♉

♂	1991	1992	1993	1994	1995	1996	1997	1998	1999	2000
JAN	1 ♉ · 21 ♊	1 ♐ · 9 ♑	1 ♋	1 ♑ · 28 ♒	1 ♍ · 23 ♌	1 ♑ · 9 ♒	1 ♍ · 3 ♎	1 ♒ · 25 ♓	1 ♎ · 26 ♏	1 ♒ · 4 ♓
FEB	1 ♊	1 ♑ · 18 ♒	1 ♋	1 ♒	1 ♌	1 ♒ · 15 ♓	1 ♎	1 ♓	1 ♏	1 ♓ · 12 ♈
MAR	1 ♊	1 ♒ · 28 ♓	1 ♋	1 ♒ · 7 ♓	1 ♌	1 ♓ · 25 ♈	1 ♎ · 9 ♍	1 ♓ · 5 ♈	1 ♏	1 ♈ · 23 ♉
APR	1 ♊ · 3 ♋	1 ♓	1 ♋ · 28 ♌	1 ♓ · 15 ♈	1 ♌	1 ♈	1 ♍	1 ♈ · 13 ♉	1 ♏	1 ♉
MAY	1 ♋ · 27 ♌	1 ♓ · 6 ♈	1 ♌	1 ♈ · 24 ♉	1 ♌ · 26 ♍	1 ♈ · 3 ♉	1 ♍	1 ♉ · 24 ♊	1 ♏ · 6 ♎	1 ♉ · 4 ♊
JUN	1 ♌	1 ♈ · 15 ♉	1 ♌ · 23 ♍	1 ♉	1 ♍	1 ♉ · 12 ♊	1 ♍ · 19 ♎	1 ♊	1 ♎	1 ♊ · 16 ♋
JUL	1 ♌ · 16 ♍	1 ♉ · 27 ♊	1 ♍	1 ♉ · 4 ♊	1 ♍ · 21 ♎	1 ♊ · 26 ♋	1 ♎	1 ♊ · 6 ♋	1 ♎ · 5 ♏	1 ♋
AUG	1 ♍	1 ♊	1 ♍ · 12 ♎	1 ♊ · 17 ♋	1 ♎	1 ♋	1 ♎ · 14 ♏	1 ♋ · 21 ♌	1 ♏	1 ♌
SEP	1 ♎	1 ♊ · 12 ♋	1 ♎ · 27 ♏	1 ♋	1 ♎ · 7 ♏	1 ♋ · 10 ♌	1 ♏ · 29 ♐	1 ♌	1 ♏ · 3 ♐	1 ♌ · 17 ♍
OCT	1 ♎ · 17 ♏	1 ♋	1 ♏	1 ♋ · 5 ♌	1 ♏ · 21 ♐	1 ♌ · 30 ♍	1 ♐	1 ♌ · 7 ♍	1 ♐ · 17 ♑	1 ♍
NOV	1 ♏ · 29 ♐	1 ♋	1 ♏ · 9 ♐	1 ♌	1 ♐ · 30 ♑	1 ♍	1 ♐ · 9 ♑	1 ♍ · 27 ♎	1 ♑ · 26 ♒	1 ♍ · 4 ♎
DEC	1 ♐	1 ♋	1 ♐ · 20 ♑	1 ♌ · 12 ♍	1 ♑	1 ♍	1 ♑ · 18 ♒	1 ♎	1 ♒	1 ♎ · 23 ♏